Should Barack Obama Be President?

DREAMS FROM MY FATHER, THE AUDACITY OF HOPE, ... Obama in '08?

W. Frederick Zimmerman

NIMBLE BOOKS LLC

NIMBLE BOOKS LLC

ISBN: 0-9788138-0-4

Copyright 2006 W. Frederick Zimmerman

Last saved **2006-10-03.**

Nimble Books LLC

2006 Medford Suite #127

Ann Arbor, MI 48104-4963

http://www.nimblebooks.com

CONTENTS

NIMBLE BOOKS LLC

BOOK DESCRIPTION

This "nimble" book provides a pithy, funny, almost schizophrenic examination of *all* the arguments that I can think of, pro and con, on the subject of Senator Barack Obama's suitability for the office of President. My promise to you is that no matter how much you already **know about O**, this book will present you with new information and new perspectives.

This is a "living" book that will be updated electronically every few months. This edition was last modified on October 17, 2006. The next update will occur in November 2006 with the addition of fifty pages devoted to analysis of *DREAMS FROM MY FATHER* and *AUDACITY OF HOPE*.

> *Current purchasers can receive future updates for free by sending proof of purchase via e-mail to obama@nimblebooks.com.*

In this book, I have relied upon the informal, rather "bulletized" house style that Nimble Books has used to produce "living books" on subjects ranging from Harry Potter and Dan Brown to science, politics, technology, and medicine. Chapters are modular to allow for easy updating and modification of the electronic master text. Favorite phrases are **bold-faced.**

Read this book if ...

- You are interested in who will be President in 2008.
- You are a Democrat.
- You are a Republican.
- You are an independent

Don't bother if ...

- You don't care what goes on in the world around you.
- You already know what you think.

KEY: HOW THIS BOOK IS LAID OUT

Each short chapter heading, like the one above, is a simple statement of fact about Barack Obama, carefully phrased to be (mostly) politically neutral: e.g. "His first name is Barack," or "He is the Senator from Illinois." Paragraphs under the first heading (for example, this one) provide more factual detail.

Pro: arguing the case that Obama should be President.

The sub-headings beginning with the word "Pro" spin the facts to support the argument that Obama should be President.

You may imagine, if you wish, that the "pros" are written by NED ROOTS, an insanely optimistic Democratic blogger.

Con: arguing the case that Obama should not be President.

The headings beginning with the word "Con" spin the facts to support the argument that Obama should *not* be President.

You may imagine, if you wish, that the "cons" are written by TROG L. O'DYTE, an intensely cynical red-meat Republican blogger.

AUTHOR'S COMMENTS

Strongly partisan readers from either party may find it objectionable to be confronted with arguments both for and against a Democratic candidate for President. If that bothers you, tune out the ones that you disagree with, and learn from the ones that you agree with. In this era of bitter partisanship, it is well to remember that there are many sides to most issues.

Careful readers may feel that some of my arguments are more plausible than others. I'll let you in on a little secret: I feel the same way. But you'll have to read between the lines to find out where I come out on the fundamental question, *Should Barack Obama Be President?*

This has been fun to write, and I think most people will learn a few things from it. Bear in mind that this is an experiment. Read the book, then tell me how you liked it! Please send email to <u>obama@nimblebooks.com</u>.

INFORMATION FROM THE PUBLISHER

Amazon Upgrade

If you purchased this book from Amazon.com, you can acquire online access via Amazon Upgrade.   Look for the link marked "Amazon Upgrade" near the picture of the book on its Amazon detail page.[1]

Buying This Book in a Bookstore

Ask the bookstore to place a special order through the Ingram catalog. Ingram prints and ships such special orders within 24 hours of receipt.

Ordering This Book for a Bookstore

Nimble Books does not provide direct fulfillment of bookseller or distributor orders.   All orders should be placed through our wholesaler, Ingram.

U.S. and International Rights

U.S. offset and international republication rights are available for this title; to discuss, please send e-mail to rights@nimblebooks.com.

Why Publish With Nimble Books?

Nimble Books LLC is an innovative publisher of timely material on topics ranging from Harry Potter and Dan Brown to politics, business, science, and medicine. We use electronic publishing technology to reach markets that are moving too fast for the large publishing conglomerates to address. Because our marketing strategy is tightly focused on the Internet, we look for titles that respond well to keyword searching in on-line markets, or to on-line promotion via blogging.

Some of our recent projects include:

- GLOBALISTAN: A GAZETTEER TO THE REMIXED WORLD OF THE 21ST CENTURY by Asia Times correspondent Pepe Escobar.

- MISQUOTES IN MISQUOTING JESUS by Dillon Burroughs

---

[1] http://www.amazon.com/dp/0978813804

- UNAUTHORIZED HARRY POTTER BOOK SEVEN NEWS

- THE SOLOMON KEY AND BEYOND

We publish twelve titles per year and we are selective. We are looking for books that are substantially "ahead of the curve" in that they address emerging trends that are readily connected with large, literate on-line communities.

We prefer manuscripts between 50,000 and 75,000 words (roughly, 150 to 225 pages) in Microsoft Word format. Please send an outline and three sample chapters to submissions@nimblebooks.com.

About Nimble Books

Our trusty Merriam-Webster Collegiate Dictionary defines "nimble" as follows:

> 1: quick and light in motion: AGILE *nimble fingers*
>
> 2 a: marked by quick, alert, clever conception, comprehension, or resourcefulness *a nimble mind* b: RESPONSIVE, SENSITIVE *a nimble listener*

And traces the etymology to the 14th Century:

> Middle English nimel, from Old English numol holding much, from niman to take; akin to Old High German neman to take, Greek nemein to distribute, manage, nomos pasture, nomos usage, custom, law

The etymology is reminiscent of the old Biblical adage, "to whom much is given, much is expected" (Luke 12:48). Nimble Books seeks to honor that Christian principle by combining the spirit of *nimbleness* with the Biblical concept of *abundance:* we deliver what you need to know about a subject in a quick, resourceful, and sensitive manner.

NIMBLE BOOKS LLC

ACKNOWLEDGEMENTS

Cheryl, Kelsey, and Parker, as always.

Barack Obama, for giving me something interesting, and worthwhile, to write about.

HIS BACKGROUND

NIMBLE BOOKS LLC

HIS FULL NAME IS "BARACK HUSSEIN OBAMA."

Con: let's face it, having a name that rhymes with "Iraq" is not a plus.

Pro: "Barack" is a cool name.

Parents all over the United States spend hours and days searching for distinctive names for their little princes. "Barack" is a hell of a lot less annoying than "Trey" or "LaTreyell."

Con: "Barack" is a goofy name.

There's only so much you can do with "Barack."

Con: The guy shares a name with Saddam Hussein. This is not helpful.

Inspired by his Muslim grandfather.

Pro: This should help him with Arab-American voters.

Although this is by no means a slam dunk. Arab Americans tend to vote more often than the median.[2]

Pro: "Obama" is a cool Kenyan name..

Con: "Obama" is a weird name.

> The original assumption was that I could never win an election statewide with a name like Barack Obama. I actually write in AUDACITY OF HOPE about a political consultant in Chicago who had originally been interested in me running statewide [who met] with me right after 9/11 and [said,] "There's a picture of [Osama] bin Laden on the magazine cover. Boy, this is really bad for you."[3]

---

[2] Zogby report, www.aaiusa.org/page/file/7822e7f9ea4990cbc1_q8m6bxau3.pdf/ 2002_AA_**Voters**.pdf

[3] *Newsweek*, September 25, 2006.

HIS FAMILY CALLS HIM "BARRY."

Pro: "Barry" sounds reassuringly normal.

To be blunt, the name "Barry" sounds he's "one of us": it sounds like he belongs to America, not to Kenya.

Con: "Barry" sounds like a twerp.

In my mind, the name "Barry" brings to mind images of an out-of-touch middle-aged Realtor[4] with graying sideburns and a burgundy jacket.

Con: those with long memories may recall Barry Goldwater.

Con: music lovers may recall Barry Manilow.

As they shriek and gibber in paroxysms of agony at the memory of some of his "hits."

Con: sports junkies with shorter memories may recall ...

- the basketball star **Rick Barry,** who was an egomaniac;
- the football star **Barry Sanders,** who was a unique talent but hardly a team leader;
- and the baseball star **Barry Bonds,** who has by most accounts earned his reputation as being perhaps the rudest person in human history.

It may seem superficial—I admit, in fact, that it *is* deeply and, offensively superficial—to throw these connotations into the mix, but as H. L. Mencken said," no one ever went broke by underestimating the intelligence of the American people". For better or worse, in the goulash of American popular culture, the name "Barry" is not an ingredient that bears the scent of successs.

---

[4] ™ The National Association of Realtors®. Idiots. Your six percent is about to go the way of the dinosaurs.

HE IS AFRICAN-AMERICAN.

In fall 2006, John McWhorter of the conservative *New York Sun* wrote an essay that neatly identified some of the touchy issues:

> ... let's imagine a white guy with all of Mr. Obama's pluses: crinkly smile, sincere concern for the little man, fine speech a couple of years ago about bringing the nation together, a certain charisma, wrote a touching autobiography. Let's call him Barrett O'Leary.

> I do not think Mr. O'Leary would be touted a year-and-change into his Senate appointment as a presidential possibility. No knock on Mr. Obama intended, mind you. ...

> The key factor that galvanizes people around the idea of Obama for president is, quite simply, that he is black. ... Take away Mr. Obama's race and he's some relatively anonymous rookie. ...

> What gives people a jolt in their gut about the idea of President Obama is the idea that it would be a ringing symbol that racism no longer rules our land. President Obama might be, for instance, a substitute for that national apology for slavery that some consider so urgent. Surely a nation with a black president would be one no longer hung up on race.

> Or not. Mr. Obama is being considered as presidential timber not despite his race, but because of it. **That is, for all of its good intentions, a dehumanization of Mr. Obama.** We're still hung up. What Mr. Obama has done is less important than his skin color and what it "means." The content of our character is not exactly center stage here. We are a long way from Selma, but not yet where the Rev. King wanted us to be.

> Yet in the grand scheme of things, I'll take a little unintended dehumanization over naked bigotry.[5]

So, deciphering the above:

---

[5] *New York Sun,* "The Color of His Skin," by John McWhorter, September 21, 2006. http://www.nysun.com/article/40050?page_no=1

Pro: An Obama Presidency would be cheaper than national reparations for slavery.

Pro: An Obama Presidency would mean white people don't have to apologize anymore.

Pro: An Obama Presidency would mean no further need for affirmative action.

Con: An Obama Presidency would mean a rookie Senator got an undeserved break.

Con: An Obama Presidency would be a form of unintended dehumanization of African-Americans.

Still, it would be better than the last four hundred years of naked bigotry!

Conspiracy-minded African Americans might not like an Obama Presidency.

According to the *New York Sun's* John McWhorter, and, **like Pope Benedict XVI, I quote:**

> Among a certain kind of black person and non-black fellow travelers — roughly, those given to surmising that the levees near the Lower Ninth Ward in New Orleans were deliberately blown up — the going wisdom would be that Mr. Obama was elected only because he is merely the kind of black person whites are "comfortable" with.[6]

It's obvious that this conspiratorial sort of thinking is, although basically idiotic, a significant part of reality. It is also true that **there are a lot of idiots out there, both black and white.** What does this line of argument imply about the desirability of an Obama Presidency?

- **Con:** an Obama Presidency would provide ammunition for idiots of all colors.

- **Pro:** an Obama Presidency would smoke out the loons.

---

[6] Ibid.

HE WAS RAISED IN HAWAII.

Pro: Hawaii is a prototype for the 21st Century USA.

Multicultural, international, diverse, Asian, patriotic, Hawaii is a prototype for the United States in the 21st Century. We could do far worse than to take a palm leaf from Hawaii's book.

Con: Hawaii is small, isolated, nonindustrial, dependent and unrepresentative.

Hawaii is simply too small, isolated, nonindustrial, and dependent on Federal largesse to be representative of the challenges faced by America in the 21st Century. We need a President who viscerally understands life in the American mainstream. Hawaii, and Obama, are fundamentally outsiders.

Pro: Hawaii has a long history of heroic politicians.

The generation of Hawaiian politicians exemplified by Daniel Inouye should make us all proud to be Americans. We could have done far worse than to have Dan Inouye as President. Hawaiians, precisely because of their geographic location and multicultural heritage, have a great tradition of valuing public services.

Pro: Hawaii is pro-Navy.

America is isolated from the rest of the world by two great oceans. America's physical security from military attack (as distinguished from *terrorist* attack) depends heavily on America's Navy.

Barack Obama grew up in Hawaii. It is impossible to live in Hawaii without picking up a strong subliminal appreciation for the importance of the U.S. Navy. Even if you are anti-military, it is still impressive to realize how many resources the Navy commands and how much importance your fellow citizens place on a strong Navy.

Con: Hawaii is heavily Democratic.

And we don't want a President from a heavily Democratic state! He might as well be from Massachusetts.

7

Pro: Hawaii is heavily Democratic

Quit whining! If President Obama is elected, it's all to the good that he should come from a heavily Democratic state. Presidents need a secure home state to be effective, not just so that they don't have to waste resources on campaigning there, but so that they have the political connections to squelch the inevitable scandal-mongering by **the vast right-wing conspiracy.**

HE WENT TO HARVARD LAW SCHOOL.

Pro: He earned it.

Yes, he had the privilege of going to Ivy League Columbia University undergraduate, but he wasn't Ryan O'Neal's Oliver Barrett IV at Harvard in *Love Story*. Barack didn't have inherited wealth or even legacy status as a stepping stone to the Ivies. He got into Columbia because he was a good student at a good preparatory school in Hawaii. Then he did well enough at Columbia that he was one of the few who achieved the highest goal for matriculating law students.

It won't do to say that his path was eased by being a minority because we're talking about Harvard here: even if he was competing in a minority pool, he was competing against the best minority students from the best colleges in the country.

Con: he has no hard skills.

The last time we had a President from an elite law school was Bill Clinton from Yale, and look how that turned out. The guy was a genius at triangulation and a complete failure when it came to action. The President of the United States does not need the same skills as elite lawyers, who, when you get right down to it, are simply parasites who facilitate transactions by doers.

Pro: He's Got Harvard intangibles

Being connected with the nation's most prestigious law school and university can only help a President to leverage the nation's most talented lawyers and scholars. The last time we had a President from an elite law school from Bill Clinton from Yale, and look what a distinguished Cabinet he put together. Clinton's Secretary of Defense Bill Cohen looks like Clausewitz compared to Bush's Donald Rumsfeld. Clinton's Treasury Secretary Richard Rubin looks like, well, Richard Rubin compared to ineffective rebel Paul O'Neill and ineffective lame duck John Snow.

Barack Obama, a pure play beneficiary of academic meritocracy, will respect the elite universities and the skills they can bring to government. Let's all hum a few tunes from *Camelot,* shall we?

OBAMA'S OK, BUT HE'S NO DEVAL PATRICK.

Deval Patrick, like Obama, is an African-American who went to Harvard Law School. *The Nation* offered this bit of lunacy on September 20, 2006:

> Barack Obama … is still the frontrunner in discussions about who might be the first African-American to occupy the Oval Office.
>
> But the voters of Massachusetts have given Obama some competition.
>
> The landslide winner of Tuesday's voting in what was supposed to be a close contest for the Democratic gubernatorial nomination, Deval Patrick, is certainly not as well known as Obama. But if, as many expect, Patrick prevails in the November election, he will quickly find a place on the national stage. [7]

Pro: Patrick has a good sense of humor.

At a rally where Obama introduced him, Patrick quipped:

> "You know your campaign is on fire when Barack Obama is your warm-up act."[8]

Con: what are they smoking at *The Nation?*

Well, we all know the answer to *that,* don't we? The chances of a Democratic governor from Massachusetts being nominated for national office are **little and less,** and Democrat should be grateful for that. Remember what happened the last time a Democratic governor from Massachusetts ran for President? Michael Dukakis **had his hat handed to him.**

Pro: the world needs more Harvard grads running things.

Deval Patrick is undeniably smart. *The Nation* compares him to Obama, "both products of challenging backgrounds who made it to Harvard Law School."

---

[7] *The Nation*, The Online Beat, "A New Star Shines from Massachusetts," September 20, 2006, http://www.thenation.com/blogs/thebeat?bid=1&pid =123247

[8] Ibid.

Con: Deval Patrick was a clerk for "one of the nation's most progressive jurists," Judge Stephen Reinhardt of *the Ninth Circuit.*

That's the federal appellate court that Focus on the Family founder James Dobson would like to abolish.[9] That single experience, regardless of the rest of Patrick's resume, pretty much guarantees that Patrick will always be a **lightning rod for cultural conservatives,** which will severely hamper any Federal ambitions Patrick may have. (Just to be clear, I think that's a shame, and the politically charged atmosphere around judicial nominations is a disgrace; but I also think it's a fact.)

It's interesting to compare Obama's track record: his jobs (community organizer, state senator) fit his Democratic agenda, but they don't make him a lightning rod. Whether by accident or design, Obama has been more successful at keeping his Federal options open than his peer Deval Patrick.

Pro: imagine an Obama-Patrick ticket!

The Nation kept on inhaling:

> But the momentum's with Patrick and, if he wins, so, too, will be the talk about a place on a future national Democratic ticket.

> Who knows? **If the America that *is* evolves to the American that *might be*,** maybe we'll see bumper stickers that read: "Obama-Patrick"? [10]

Con: Democrats don't realize that this sort of fantasizing makes them appear *way* too desperate.

Patrick hasn't even been elected to office. Obama has been in office for less than two years.

Con: Why *should* there be a double-minority ticket?

It doesn't really make sense to talk about an Obama-Patrick ticket as if that would somehow prove that America is an egalitarian wonderland. In a nation

---

[9] Kevin Phillips, *American Theocracy.*

[10] *The Nation,* ibid.

with a representative political system, having two national candidates from the same **small minority (12.8%)** should be cause for concern, not cause for celebration.   The odds of such a paired ticket occurring randomly are about 1 in 64, or less than 2%.

HIS WIFE HAS A BETTER-PAYING JOB THAN HE DOES.

During 2005, Obama's income as a public official almost tripled to $154,047, after he left the Illinois state Senate for the nation's capital. His wife [Michelle's] income as an administrator at the not-for-profit University of Chicago Hospitals nearly tripled to $316,962, from $121,910.

The Obamas' salaries took their sizable jumps roughly at the same time in early 2005. The senator started his six-year term as senator in January; his wife was promoted to the hospitals' vice president for community and external affairs in March.

Obama said in an interview last week with The Associated Press that his wife, who, like him, is a Harvard law school graduate, was deserving of the promotion and raise.

"You can't fault her for being smarter and better qualified for all sorts of jobs than I am," he said. "She shouldn't be penalized for that."[11]

Pro: his wife is smart.

Obama married up. Good for him!

Con: that's a pretty big coincidence that she got a 300% raise right after her husband became a U.S. Senator.

I hope my wife becomes a U.S. Senator soon.

Con: she got the raise because she went to Princeton and Harvard.

In explaining her salary increase, Easton and a spokesman for the senator both stressed her educational background, which includes an undergraduate degree from Princeton and a law degree from Harvard.[12]

---

[11] Associated Press, "Obamas' 2005 reported income nearly 1.7 million," September 25, 2006.

Well, *that's* all right, then.

Con: all the other hospital vice presidents are obscenely overpaid, too.

> Hospitals spokesman John Easton said Obama's salary was in line with the compensation received by the not-for-profit medical center's 16 other vice presidents.
>
> A tax return for the hospitals covering the 12 months ended June 30, 2005, shows most of the hospital center's vice presidents earning between $291,000 and $362,000.[13]

Well, *that's* all right, then.

Seriously, can you believe how much money these stupid hospital executives make when most people in this country are struggling with steadily increasing costs of health care? I don't have a problem with *doctors* being highly paid, but, c'mon: **hospital executive = paperpusher.**

Pro: Michelle Obama seems to have good common sense.

> Easton said the hospitals' management had discussed a promotion to vice president with Obama previously but that she had been reluctant to undertake the commitment until her husband's Senate campaign had finished. In part, she wanted to wait until her family had made a decision on whether to maintain their primary residence in Illinois, which they did, and she had a better sense of the demands on her time as a senator's wife, he said.[14]

I really can't quibble with this. Good on her!

---

[12] *Chicago Tribune*, "Officials explain increase in Michelle Obama's salary", Mike Dorning, September 26, 2006.

[13] Ibid.

[14] Ibid.

What he's done

HE GAVE THE KEYNOTE SPEECH AT THE 2004 DEMOCRATIC CONVENTION.

The full text of Obama's keynote speech may be found at the address below.[15]

Pro: He was inspiring.

> there's not a liberal America and a conservative America -- there's the United States of America. There's not a black America and white America and Latino America and Asian America; there's the United States of America. The pundits like to slice-and-dice our country into Red States and Blue States; Red States for Republicans, Blue States for Democrats. **But I've got news for them, too. We worship an awesome God in the Blue States, and we don't like federal agents poking around our libraries in the Red States.** We coach Little League in the Blue States and have gay friends in the Red States. There are patriots who opposed the war in Iraq and patriots who supported it. We are one people, all of us pledging allegiance to the stars and stripes, all of us defending the United States of America.

Damn fine words that will be long remembered. It's hard to imagine writing a history of this period without referring to this speech, if only because Barack Obama did such a fine job of capturing the elusive (illusive?) spirit of national unity.

Con: He mentioned John Kerry 13 times.

> Our party has chosen a man to lead us who embodies the best this country has to offer. That man is **John Kerry.**

> **John Kerry** understands the ideals of community, faith, and sacrifice, because they've defined his life.

> **John Kerry** believes in an America where hard work is rewarded.

> **John Kerry** believes in an America where all Americans can afford the same health coverage our politicians in Washington have for themselves

---

[15] http://www.pbs.org/newshour/vote2004/demconvention/speeches/-obama.html

John **Kerry** believes in energy independence, so we aren't held hostage to the profits of oil companies or the sabotage of foreign oil fields.

John **Kerry** believes in the constitutional freedoms that have made our country the envy of the world, and he will never sacrifice our basic liberties nor use faith as a wedge to divide us.

And John **Kerry** believes that in a dangerous world, war must be an option, but it should never be the first option.

We have real enemies in the world. These enemies must be found. They must be pursued and they must be defeated. John **Kerry** knows this.

And just as Lieutenant **Kerry** did not hesitate to risk his life to protect the men who served with him in Vietnam, President **Kerry** will not hesitate one moment to use our military might to keep America safe and secure.

. Do we participate in a politics of cynicism or a politics of hope? **John Kerry** calls on us to hope.

John **Kerry** believes in America.

.. if we do what we must do, then I have no doubt that all across the country, from Florida to Oregon, from Washington to Maine, the people will rise up in November, and John **Kerry** will be sworn in as president...

Didn't happen, did it? And thank God for that. What a disaster Kerry would have been. That becomes clearer with every passing day.

Pro: he's aware that Kerry is a bit of an upper-class loon.

At the Gridiron White House correspondents' dinner in 2006, he commented:

It's great to be at the Gridiron dinner. Wow, What an extravaganza! Men in tails. Women in gowns. An orchestra playing, as folks reminisce about the good old days. Kind of like dinner at the Kerrys.

Pro: Barack Obama presciently warned us against Four More Years of Bush

John Kerry may be a wimp, but he would have been a much better President than **four more years of Cheney and Curious George.**

He has been elected as a United States Senator.

Pro: He's a member of the most exclusive club in the world.

There's no other elected office, except President, with power quite as rarefied as the power that attaches to a United States Senator. Senate rules allow you to block any legislation with a simple word. Rich people want to befriend you. Your terms are six years long, so you actually have time to enjoy your clout.

Con: He's not a governor.

No Senator has been elected for President since John F. Kennedy in 1960. There are good reasons for that: as a Senator, you are just one of a hundred, and you are hemmed in with frustrating constraints: you build a record on speeches instead of executive actions, you have to negotiate to get *anything* done, and worst, **those pesky votes keep you away from fund-raising,**

Con: He became a United States Senator by beating Alan Keyes.

That's like beating the '62 Mets, or, (sob), the **2003 Tigers.**

HIS CAMPAIGN FINANCES ARE UNUSUAL.

This page, from the Center for Responsive Politics, gives an overview of Obama's campaign finances. What does this information tell us about whether Barack Obama should be President?

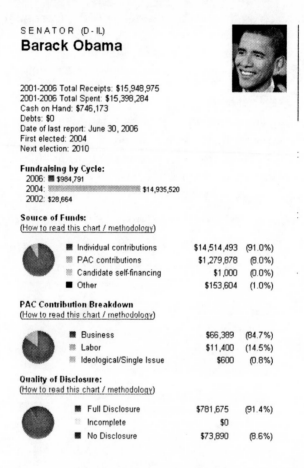

SENATOR (D-IL)
Barack Obama

2001-2006 Total Receipts: $15,948,975
2001-2006 Total Spent: $15,398,284
Cash on Hand: $746,173
Debts: $0
Date of last report: June 30, 2006
First elected: 2004
Next election: 2010

Fundraising by Cycle:
2006: $984,791
2004: $14,935,520
2002: $28,664

Source of Funds:
(How to read this chart / methodology)

Individual contributions	$14,514,493	(91.0%)
PAC contributions	$1,279,878	(8.0%)
Candidate self-financing	$1,000	(0.0%)
Other	$153,604	(1.0%)

PAC Contribution Breakdown
(How to read this chart / methodology)

Business	$66,389	(84.7%)
Labor	$11,400	(14.5%)
Ideological/Single Issue	$600	(0.8%)

Quality of Disclosure:
(How to read this chart / methodology)

Full Disclosure	$781,675	(91.4%)
Incomplete	$0	
No Disclosure	$73,890	(8.6%)

Pro: he's a very cost-effective campaigner.

The dude only spent $1,000 of his own money on becoming a U.S. Senator. When you look at the tens of millions of dollars that some **total gasbags** have spent and *not* become Senators, this makes Obama look like a genius. It's going to take campaign genius for a liberal Democrat from the big city (Chicago) to beat the Republicans.

Con: he's too cheap to be President.

Let's say I'm running for Senate. Hey, to make it feel real, let's make it just for *state* Senate. I tell you that I am willing to invest a whopping $1,000 of my own money in the project. How would *you* vote? This looks like someone who's got a bad case of **OPM: Other People's Money.**

HE HAD A WELL PUBLICIZED CLASH WITH JOHN MCCAIN.

Senator John McCain sent Obama **a deeply sarcastic letter** on February 6, 2006, upset because Obama had supported a Democratic ethics reform bill instead of McCain's bipartisan effort.

> I'm embarrassed to admit that after all these years in politics I failed to interpret your previous assurances as typical rhetorical gloss routinely used in politics to make self-interested partisan posturing appear more noble. Again, sorry for the confusion, but please be assured I won't make the same mistake again.[16]

Obama and McCain patched things up, but the event was still fresh in Obama's mind at the Gridiron Club dinner in March 2006.

> And speaking of Senator McCain.

> This whole ethics thing has been an adventure. I was really excited when they asked me to be the lead Democratic spokesman. But I don't know. Turns out, it's a little like being given the Kryptonite concession at a Superman convention. I mean, how did I know it was a freshman hazing? It gets a little depressing. So as I sometimes do when I get a little down, I wrote a song. Maestro?

> *(To the tune of "If I Only Had a Brain")*

> *I'm aspiring to greatness, but somehow I feel weightless*

> *A freshman's sad refrain*

> *I could be a great uniter, making ethics rules much tighter*

> *If I only had McCain*

> *I could bring us all together, no storm we couldn't weather,*

---

[16] http://mccain.senate.gov/index.cfm?fuseaction=NewsCenter.—
ViewPressRelease&Content_id=1654

We'd feel each other's pain

Red and blue wouldn't matter, party differences would shatter

If I only had McCain

Oh why is it so hard, for honest men of good will to agree,

If we ever found a way to strike a deal, would we survive... politically?

When a wide-eyed young idealist, confronts a seasoned realist

There's bound to be some strain

With the game barely started, I'd be feeling less downhearted

If I only had McCain

Still I hope for the better, though I may rewrite my letter

Cause I gotta have McCain

Needless to say, my Grammy was in the spoken word category!

I should say that I really do get along well with Senator McCain. But as you know, not everyone in politics does. Because of his superstar status, his virtuous image, the kind of hero worship treatment he gets from all of you, some of my colleagues call John a prima donna. Me? I call him a role model. (Think of it as affirmative action. Why should the white guys be the only ones who are overhyped?)[17]

---

[17] http://blogs.suntimes.com/sweet/2006/03/best_of_gridiron_obama_lynne_c.html

HE'S WRITTEN A BEST-SELLING BOOK.

[In 2005 b]ook royalties and advances brought in about $1.2 million for the senator-author whose first book, an autobiography published about a decade ago, became a best-seller during his 2004 campaign.[18]

Sales Rank History

Current Rank	7-Day Average	30-Day Average	90-Day Average	Lifetime Average	Best Rank	Worst Rank
1,524	1,694	1,539	2,055	1,080	13	4,838

Figure 1. Amazon sales ranks for *Dreams From My Father*, November 2004 - September 2006, via Titlez.com.[19]

Pro: not only is he a U.S. Senator, but he's also a best-selling author.

Pro: there is a long history of Senators being authors.

John F. Kennedy, Gary Hart, John McCain ...

Con: isn't this kind of piling on? How much good fortune does one man deserve?

---

[18] Associated Press, "Obamas' 2005 reported income nearly 1.7 million," September 25, 2006.

[19] http://www.titlez.com/app/oneSheet.aspx?ASIN=1400082773

HE WON A GRAMMY.

Obama won the 2005 Grammy for Best Spoken Word Album for his audio recording of *Dreams of My Father*.[20]

Pro: he beat out Sean Penn, Al Franken, George Carlin, and Garrison Keillor.

At least three of the competitors that Obama beat out are bona fide geniuses of the spoken word, and Sean Penn is a genius of the grunt.

Con: He's no Orrin Hatch.

Obama's not a real artist like the lyricist/Senator from Utah.

Con: He didn't even pick up the Grammy until September 2006.

> the Illinois Democrat was unable to attend the ceremony due to the demands of his day job. On Wednesday, Obama finally got the golden statue in his hands during the annual Grammys on the Hill Day, an event in Washington D.C. by the National Academy of Recording Arts & Sciences where diverse members of the music-making community are brought in to impress upon lawmakers the importance of the industry in American life.[21]

A man who has so little respect for the musical community is clearly unfit to be President.

Con: He was upstaged by Kelly Clarkson.

> "American Idol" winner Kelly Clarkson was the star attraction Wednesday, as she and her band transformed one of the halls on Capitol Hill into a studio to record her new song, "Believe." On one of the two takes recorded, eight lawmakers helped the rhythm section by clapping along, reports Reuters.

---

[20] http://www.grammy.com/GRAMMY_Awards/Annual_Show/ 48_nominees.aspx

[21] http://www.eurweb.com/story/eur28499.cfm

According to the House Historian's Office, Clarkson's action marks the first time the Cannon House Office Building Caucus Room has been used to record a song.[22]

If you can't upstage Kelly Clarkson, you're no better than Taylor Hicks. And you don't deserve to be President.

---

[22] http://www.eurweb.com/story/eur28499.cfm

HE VISITED AFRICA IN AUGUST 2006.

Senator Obama visited Africa in August 2006 and went to South Africa, Chad, and his father's homeland, Kenya.

Pro: He's a mensch.

Here are a few of the things Senator Obama did on his summer vacation:

1. Attended a ceremony the 200 people (both American and Kenyan) who died in the 1988 bombing of the U.S. Embassy.

2. Encouraged the South African government to respond more effectively to HIV/AIDS.

3. Urged Kenya's government to end corruption.

4. Along with his wife, took a public HIV/AIDS test.

5. Visited a malaria research institute.

6. Visited a program helping children who have been orphaned by AIDS.

7. Visited his grandmother.

8. Apologized to his grandmother for all the attention she has received because of him.[23]

That's a hell of a lot better than I do on my vacations.

Con: who cares? It's Africa.

If we're going to go with a President from a non-European background, let's go with one whose relatives are from a country whose friendship will actually help us, like China or India.

Pro: Kenyans Love Him.

> ... a crowd on the street outside chanted "Obama, come to us" and waved banners bearing his likeness. And when he arrived in Kogelo last Saturday in a

---

[23] *Time*, "What Barack Obama Can Do for Africa – And Vice Versa", August 28, 2006. http://www.time.com/time/nation/article/0,8599,1423977,00.html

motorcade followed by camera crews and reporters, screaming crowds chanted his name, a praise singer catalogued his strengths and children sang songs about him they had written especially for the occasion. [24]

Con: Who cares? It's Kenya.

Bill Clinton gets cheering crowds everywhere he goes in Africa. Barack Obama only gets cheered in Kenya. Kenya is a good country, but it is not even the most important country in Africa, and there are 53 other countries there.

---

[24] *Time*, "What Barack Obama Can Do for Africa – And Vice Versa", August 28, 2006. http://www.time.com/time/nation/article/0,8599,1423977,00.html

HE ANGERED SOME OFFICIALS IN KENYA BY CRITICIZING THAT NATION'S CORRUPTION.

During his trip, Obama pointedly encouraged Kenyan officials to do more to fight corruption at an Aug. 28 speech in Nairobi:

> ... It's more than just history and outside influences that explain why Kenya lags behind. Like many nations across this continent, where Kenya is failing is in its ability to create a government that is transparent and accountable. One that serves its people and is free from corruption.
>
> There is no doubt that what Kenyans have accomplished with this independence is both impressive and inspiring. ...
>
> And yet, the reason I speak of the freedom that you fought so hard to win is because today that freedom is in jeopardy. It is being threatened by corruption.
>
> Corruption is not a new problem. It's not just a Kenyan problem, or an African problem. It's a human problem, and it has existed in some form in almost every society. My own city of Chicago has been the home of some of the most corrupt local politics in American history, from patronage machines to questionable elections. In just the last year, our own U.S. Congress has seen a representative resign after taking bribes, and several others fall under investigation for using their public office for private gain.
>
> But while corruption is a problem we all share, here in Kenya it is a crisis - a crisis that's robbing an honest people of the opportunities they have fought for - the opportunity they deserve....
>
> It is painfully obvious that corruption stifles development - it siphons off scarce resources that could improve infrastructure, bolster education systems, and strengthen public health. It stacks the deck so high against entrepreneurs that they cannot get their job-creating ideas off the ground. In fact, one recent survey showed that corruption in Kenya costs local firms 6% of their revenues, the difference between good-paying jobs in Kenya or somewhere else. And corruption also erodes the state from the inside out, sickening the justice

system until there is no justice to be found, poisoning the police forces until their presence becomes a source of insecurity rather than comfort.

Corruption has a way of magnifying the very worst twists of fate. It makes it impossible to respond effectively to crises -- whether it's the HIV/AIDS pandemic or malaria or crippling drought.

What's worse - corruption can also provide opportunities for those who would harness the fear and hatred of others to their agenda and ambitions.

... In the end, if the people cannot trust their government to do the job for which it exists - to protect them and to promote their common welfare - all else is lost. And this is why the struggle against corruption is one of the great struggles of our time.

The good news is that there are already signs of progress here...[25]

Con: Obama offended Kenya!

Evidently Obama's remarks stung some Kenyan officials, for soon after his departure Kenya's ambassador-designate to the United States, Peter Oginga Ogego, sent Obama a scathing official complaint:

I hereby wish to communicate to you the displeasure and disappointment of the Government of Kenya, (Kenyan) Embassy in Washington DC, and majority of Kenyans, with regards to your recent utterances while in Kenya.

"Your unprovoked and uncalled for statements were in bad taste, particularly given that your visit was well arranged in advance, with full briefings given to your office in Washington DC by the Kenya Embassy.

... You deliberately, without real cause or reason, other than what appears (to be) to seek cheap publicity and inconsequential populism, chose to publicly attack the democratically elected Government of Kenya, in total disregard for the requisite protocol and acceptable methods to address the issues you raised, what with programmed appointments to meet Cabinet Ministers and even the Head of State, since your visit was official.

---

[25] http://obama.senate.gov/speech/060828-an_honest_gover nment_a_hopeful_future/index.html

... Rather than appreciate and even encourage the gallant and heroic efforts that our Government and Kenyans have put in dismantling the deeply embedded networks and chains of corruption, you carelessly, in a manner akin to political activism, chose to trash and sneer at us""[26]

Pro: Obama doesn't take any crap.

His Sep. 20 reply to Ambassador Ogego is classic.[27] Nutshell summary:"**I'm smarter and classier than you.**" I've included a translation.

Dear Ambassador Ogego,

Thank you for your letter, outlining the concerns of the Government of Kenya on my visit to your country last month. I appreciate hearing from you on this important matter. First, I want to thank you and your colleagues in Government for hosting my visit.

The officials with whom I met were engaging and insightful and, like me, interested in promoting a strong relationship between our two nations.

Moreover, I appreciate the time and energy the Government devoted to ensuring that my visit was a success.

Concerning your letter, under ordinary circumstances, I would happily respond in kind to each point you raise as well as the charges levelled by Dr Alfred Mutua, the Government Spokesperson.

However, because the accusations are so ad hominem and groundless, I feel it would be more productive to simply issue a general response.

[You are an idiot.]

I invite you to follow up with me in person or via further correspondence issues that you feel warrant additional attention.

[So that I can personally throw your letter directly into the circular file.]

---

[26] http://allafrica.com/stories/200609020064.html

[27] http://allafrica.com/stories/printable/200609210036.html

I am disappointed that you believe my speech at the University of Nairobi on August 28 was breach of protocol. This goes against the best traditions of free expression that both of our nations hold so dear.

[You are an idiot.]

It also cuts against the advice President Kibaki dispensed during our meeting - that the relationship between the United States and Kenya is so strong that we should simply bring forward issues of concern, rather than let them fester beneath the surface.

[You are an idiot.]

Moreover, as a technical matter, it is my understanding that, at the time your letter was issued, you had not yet presented your credentials to President Bush, making your protest a breach of protocol.

[You are a protocol-violating idiot.]

But again, we need not concern ourselves with such trivial matters –

[Although I just spent four paragraphs doing just that.]

it is far more constructive to engage in an exchange of ideas than to stand on protocol.

[Although I just spent four paragraphs doing just that.]

The overwhelming majority of your comments appear to take issue with my speech. Let me say in unequivocal terms that I stand behind every word of my speech at the University of Nairobi.

[You are an idiot.]

My speech was a challenge to both our great nations. On the one hand, it challenged my country to formulate a more intelligent and effective foreign policy that better addresses the needs of the Kenyan people.

[American Republicans are a bunch idiots, too. Obama in '08!]

On the other hand, it called on your country, especially the leaders of all political parties, to make the internal reforms, such as ending corruption and tribalism, needed to bring greater prosperity to the intelligent and hardworking people of Kenya.

As I noted in my speech, Kenya is to be commended for its many accomplishments: A robust democracy, a vibrant civil society and the lack of major ethnic violence.

One has only to look at the uneven early history of the United States, which included the scrapping of the Articles of Confederation and a bloody Civil War, to appreciate the progress Kenya has made to date.

But, if Kenya is to meet the challenges of the 21st Century and satisfy the aspirations of its great people, substantially more progress must be made on the issues of tribalism and corruption.

While you **seem to** believe that the Government is doing all it can,

[You're either an idiot, or a liar.]

a number of Kenyan politicians, members of civil society, the media and many "ordinary" Kenyans have told me the exact opposite. Many have welcomed my statements as a much-needed call to action.

I leave it to the people of Kenya - not the Government or any political party - to pass final judgment on the accuracy and utility of my speech.

[Not you.]

From Article 98 to agricultural subsidies, I plan on working to shape a more intelligent, effective US foreign policy.

[More agricultural subsidies, that's what US foreign policy needs!]

I will also continue working with my colleagues in the US Senate to combat corruption, which affects all societies, as I made clear in my speech.

You may have noticed that, during my time in Africa, a controversy in the US developed around a Bill I am pushing to increase the transparency of US Government spending.

For the sake of the Knyan people, I hope that your Government is willing to make progress on the critical issue of corruption, and on the issue of tribalism as well.

Again, I appreciate this opportunity to exchange views with you. I look forward to more direct discussions concerning these critical issues.

Thank you again for a wonderful and memorable visit.

lo this again soon.]

romptly rallied to support Obama.

various political and religious leaders have rallied behind US Senator Mr Barack Obama, saying he spoke the truth about endemic corruption and tribalism in Kenya.

Former Planning Minister Prof Anyang' Nyong'o, Health Assistant Minister Dr Enock Kibungunchy, nominated MP Mr Kipkalya Kones, Nyakach MP Mr Peter Odoyo, secretary of Rift Valley Alliance Mr Simon Lilan and Maseno South Bishop Rev Francis Abiero Mwai said the Illinois senator spoke what was in the domain of Kenyans.

They wondered why Kenya's envoy to the US would defend the obvious. Nyong'o said the problem facing Kenyans at the moment was how to remove the current regime in order to tackle corruption and tribalism.[28]

---

[28] *The Standard* (Kenya), September 22, 2006.

34

WHAT HE STANDS FOR

HE SUPPORTS TRANSPARENCY IN GOVERNMENT SPENDING.

Together with Oklahoma Senator Jim Coburn, Obama co-**sponsored S. 2590, "A bill to require full disclosure of all entities and organizations receiving Federal funds."**[29] The bill requires creation of a website with a freely searchable database of all entities receiving Federal funds—including, most notably, entities receiving Congressional earmarks. The bill was signed into law in September 2006.

Pro: this is logical, cost-efficient, and sensible.

A future President *should* be committed to transparency in government spending.

Con: he's spoiling the fun for everyone else.

As one Congresscritter observed, "One man's pork is another man's beef."

Without Congressional earmarks, where would we be? In a strange, dangerous land where Members of Congress could not rely on earmarked appropriations to do favors for friends and entrench themselves in office.

Pro: this is patriotic.

Section 3 of the act specifically excludes classified information from the act's purview, so there is no danger that the Coburn-Obama Act will gore any sacred bulls.

---

[29] http://thomas.loc.gov/cgi-bin/bdquery/z?d109:s.02590:

HE IS AGAINST CLUSTER-BOMBING CIVILIANS.

Obama was one of 30 U.S. Senators who voted in favor of : S.Amdt. 4882 to H.R. 5631, an amendment whose purpose was "to protect civilian lives from unexploded cluster munitions."[30]

Pro: Obama has a heart.

As the *Irregular Times* blog put it,

> I don't think it's too much to ask of Presidential candidates that they support a few simple basic moral values. For instance, I think it's reasonable to expect that politicians who run for President of the United States do not support dropping cluster bombs on areas of concentrated civilian populations, and then leaving unexploded cluster bombs behind for children to pick up and play with until they explode.[31]

Con: Obama has a bleeding heart.

This is **classic liberal grand-standing.** Does this legislation apply to Hezbollah or Iran? Does this legislation prohibit suicide bombers from using the extremely inhumane technique of adding chemical and bacteriological weapons to bombs filled with nails? No, of course not. This bill attempts to punish Israel for using effective weapons against targets that are hidden in civilian populations—in other words, it attempts to prohibit Israel from using cluster weapons at all. This is the worst sort of **namby-pambyism,** attempting to impose symbolic rules of restraint on war, an inherently violent and brutal process.

---

[30] http://www.senate.gov/legislative/LIS/roll_call_lists/roll_call_vote_cfm.cfm?congress=109&session=2&vote=00232

[31] http://irregulartimes.com/index.php/archives/2006/09/15/cluster-bombs-2008/

HE SUPPORTS HEALTH BENEFITS FOR GAY CIVIL PARTNERS.

In his floor statement on the Federal Marriage Amendment, Senator Obama staked out his position on marriage rights for gays:

> I realize that for some Americans, this is an important issue. And I should say that personally, I do believe that marriage is between a man and a woman.
>
> But let's be honest. That's not what this debate is about. Not at this time.
>
> This debate is an attempt to break a consensus that is quietly being forged in this country...
>
> It's a consensus between a majority of Americans who say, "You know what, maybe some of us are comfortable with gay marriage right now and some of us are not. **But most of us do believe that gay couples should be able to visit each other in the hospital and share health care benefits; most of us do believe that they should be treated with dignity and have their privacy respected by the federal government.**" [32]

Pro: Obama's position is sensitive to the rights of gay people.

Health care benefits for partners is a huge issue. Keeping the federal government and the U.S. Constitution out of the marriage debate is a huge win for supporters of gay and lesbian rights.

> I agree with most Americans, with Democrats and Republicans, with Vice President Cheney, with over 2,000 religious leaders of all different beliefs, that decisions about marriage, as they always have, should be left to the states. [33]

---

[32] http://obama.senate.gov/speech/060605-floor_statement_of_senator_bar ack_obama_on_the_federal_marriage_amendment/index.html

[33] Ibid.

Con: Obama's position doesn't go far enough in respecting the rights of gay people.

So, Senator, if a gay couple looked you in the eye and said "do you believe we should be married?" what would you say to them? Would you say:

> ...personally, I do believe that marriage is between a man and a woman.[34]

Doesn't that strike you as insulting?

Con: Obama's falsely claiming a non-existent consensus.

Consensus means we all agree. We *don't* all agree. Many sincere and well-meaning people believe exactly the opposite of your claimed consensus and do not believe that the government should enforce civil rights for gay marriages.

If we don't have a consensus, what do we have? We have a group trying to assemble a majority to enforce its views, that's what we have. And unfortunately for your side, most of the time that marriage comes up in an election, the side favoring "traditional" marriage wins.

Pro: Obama wants us to spend our time more constructively.

> So don't tell me that this is the best use of our time. Don't tell me that this is what people want to see talked about on TV and in the newspapers all day. We wonder why the American people have such a low opinion of Washington these days. This is why.
>
> **We are better than this.** And we certainly owe the American people more than this. I know that this amendment will fail, and when it does, I hope we can start discussing issues and offering proposals that will actually improve the lives of most Americans.[35]

I for one whole-heartedly agree that there are more constructive issues that we should all be debating. Now, if only both progressives and conservatives will agree to take marriage off the table, we can really get somewhere...

---

[34] Ibid.

[35] Ibid.

Con: a federal amendment making marriage between a man and a woman would allow states to spend their energies more wisely.

Maybe the best thing is for gay and lesbian rights advocates to stop asking for civil legitimacy and focus their energies on universal health care for all...

HE BELIEVES IN ENERGY INDEPENDENCE.

Sep. 19, Washington, DC -- Sen. Barack Obama (D-Ill.) will outline a plan for making America less dependent on foreign oil in a speech to MoveOn members aimed at mobilizing the organization's volunteers and voters in the upcoming congressional elections. His speech will focus on the need to promote clean, renewable sources of energy to protect national security and the environment.

Obama's speech is the second in a three-part "Progressive Vision" series sponsored by MoveOn to promote the top three issues of concern to its members in this fall's political battle over the country's direction.[36]

Pro: energy independence through clean, renewable energy would be a good thing.

And Obama is in favor of it!

Con: this is Obama pandering to the most impractical elements of the Democratic party.

If the Democratic party has a prayer of winning the *Presidential* election in 2008, its potentially viable candidates need to stay as far away from MoveOn as possible.

Clean, renewable energy would be nice. However, renewable sources of energy have an awkward habit of being, well, ugly. **Have you ever seen a wind farm?** Ok, now imagine ten million of them. Presto, energy independence!

Pro: he names names.

"For someone who talks tough about defending America, actually solving our energy crisis seems pretty low on the president's agenda," said Obama at a Georgetown University speech sponsored by MoveOn.org.

"And that's because as much as George Bush might want to defend America, he also needs to defend his vision of government, and that's a

---

[36] U.S. Newswire, Sep. 19, 2006

government that can't, won't and shouldn't solve great national challenges like our energy dependence," he added.

... Obama said Bush has not gone far enough to follow-up on his remark in the State of the Union Address that America is "addicted to oil."

"It is not enough to acknowledge the problem," Obama said. "There are still another 11 steps in the 12-step program."

Con: Obama is too kind.

We need a Democratic President who will have the *cojones* to point out that Bush is **a thrall of the oil industry.**

Con: Obama can't count.

Bush is actually all the way through the third step of the twelve-step program for overcoming energy addiction.

1. We admitted we were <u>powerless</u> over our addiction - that our lives had become unmanageable

2. Came to <u>believe</u> that a Power greater than ourselves could restore us to sanity

[ExxonMobil.]

3. Made a <u>decision</u> to turn our will and our lives over to the care of God as we understood God

4. Made a searching and fearless <u>moral inventory</u> of ourselves.

[This is the one where George seems to have run into trouble.]

HE WANTS DETROIT TO BUILD MORE HYBRIDS.

Obama's solution to Detroit's woes calls for a government "deal" with the "Big Three."

> Obama highlighted legislative proposals he has offered. They include a "bargain" with the big three automakers that would help them with their high retiree health costs if they use the savings to invest in fuel efficient cars.[37]

Con: Obama can't count. It's the Big Two now.

Con: so Uncle Sam's going to pick up the General's retiree health costs?

There's a horrible idea.

Con: Obama thinks *hybrids* are killing Detroit.

> Citing job cuts at Ford Motor Co., Obama said the U.S. auto industry is hurting because it has failed to keep pace with foreign automakers who are transitioning much faster to sales of hybrid and other efficient cars.[38]

This is so wrong it's scary. Hybrids are only a tiny fraction of the market. Unfortunately, there are two primary reasons imports sell better: higher quality and lower manufacturing costs.

> He also called for higher fuel efficiency standards, greater ethanol production and making E-85 pumps widely available, noting that less than 700 of the nation's 170,000 gas stations sell the blend of 85 percent ethanol and 15 percent gasoline.[39]

---

[37] Environment & Energy News, September 20, 2006.

[38] Ibid.

[39] Ibid.

Con: Obama can't count.

> Obama also urged U.S. automakers to produce more flex-fuel cars that can run on blended gasoline. "It is time for them to install those tanks in every single car they make, **and it is time for the government to cover this small cost**," he said.

There's no such thing as a small cost when you are talking about mandating a feature on every single car manufactured in America.

HE'S AGAINST EPILEPSY.

Senator Obama spoke at a function for Citizens United for Research In Epilepsy in March 2005.

Con: scarcely a daring position for an elected official!

Pro: I was touched by his empathy for the families.

> I've thought about three mothers, sitting around a kitchen table, sharing the pain and the helplessness that go along with watching the child you love, the child whose happiness you live for, struggle with a disease that mom and dad can't fix. A disease that doesn't necessarily go away with the doctor's medicine, that isn't talked about most nights on the news, that isn't funded and recognized like a lot of the other diseases.[40]

Pro: I learned something important from his speech.

> Just last week, USA Today reported that hundreds of U.S. soldiers are returning from Iraq with a condition known as traumatic brain injury, or TBI. Even though new technology and better body armor are helping them survive bomb and rocket attacks, the blasts are still causing these soldiers brain damage. As of January, 437 cases have been diagnosed in Army hospitals alone, and some doctors are saying that it could become the "signature wound of the Iraq war."
>
> **As some of you may know, TBI is the greatest risk factor for developing epilepsy.** In fact, a study of Vietnam vets showed that 51 percent of those who suffered TBI went on to develop the disease....

Pro: and Obama drew the right conclusion from it.

> We simply cannot tell our heroes that when it comes to dealing with TBI or epilepsy, they're on their own.[41]

---

[40] http://obama.senate.gov/speech/050311-cure_keynote_address/index.html

[41] Ibid.

Pro: he knows how to rally a community.

> ... we do have a growing community that is on the march. We have allies in government who know that we can defeat this disease if we work together. And we have the hope that every parent has for their child.
>
> The hope you have the first time you bring them to the doctor's office, and you just want them to walk out with some medicine and a lollipop. The hope you have the first day you watch them get on the bus, when you want them to fit in with the rest of the kids and do well in school. The hope you have the day of their first job, when you want them to call you and let you know how great it went. The hope you have when they walk down the aisle, when you want nothing more than for them to find love and happiness in life.
>
> These are hopes we hold not only for our own children, but for every parent and every child every where. And if we leave here tonight determined to turn those hopes into action, into a sustained commitment to fight epilepsy that's more than just about one fundraiser or one benefit, we will find a cure and we will keep hope alive for millions of families for generations to come. Thank you, and God Bless you.[42]

America needs a lot of rallying right now. We could do much worse than to elect this man.

---

[42] Ibid.

He supports veterans' rights.

I was surprised to learn that Obama spoke at an American Legion conference in March 2005 shortly after President Bush proposed a budget that included cuts in veterans' health benefits.

Pro: he showed that he *gets* it about veterans.

My touchstone for understanding veterans' rights is Robert A. Heinlein's *Starship Troopers,* the classic science fiction novel in which only veterans get to vote. Obama said two things in this speech that showed me he has a Heinleinesque appreciation for veterans:

> [When I first heard about this budget] I thought about my grandfather, who signed up for duty in World War II the day after Pearl Harbor. He marched across Europe in Patton's army, and when he came home, it was the education and opportunity offered by the GI Bill that allowed his family to build their own American Dream. [43]

And:

> The President never hesitates to praise the service of our veterans and acknowledge the debt we owe them for their service, and I commend him for that. Now I hope he will renew his commitment by increasing funding for the VA, and ensure that our veterans receive more than just words of praise, but also the health care and benefits they've earned.[44]

Right on!

Con: he's a politician, of course he supports veterans' entitlements.

The closer you look at this guy, the more he looks like an old-fashioned Chicago pol who never met an entitlement he didn't like.

---

[43] http://obama.senate.gov/speech/050328-obama_remarks_to_the_
american_legion_legislative_rally/index.html

[44] Ibid.

HE WANTS DEMOCRATS TO "CLOSE THE DEAL."

Obama's Sep. 18 speech to the Iowa caucus caused an intense and protracted controversy on the Democratic blog *Dailykos*.

Con: He implicitly criticized other Democrats.

The thread-starter, **SusanG,** objected to these two sentences in his speech:

> "What Democrats have to do is to close the deal. We have got to show we have a serious agenda for change."[45]

SusanG argued that this choice of words showed bad judgment by casting Democrats in a defensive light. She would have preferred that he say:

> Democrats **can** close the deal **because** we have a serious agenda for change.[46]

Bottom line: she wants Obama to be more careful about what he says.

> He said those two sentences, and it happens that this kind of language leads to exactly the kind of problem we're trying to get away from -- the idea that we're a party that **can't** close a deal and **can't** show a serious agenda.

Follow the footnotes[47] to read the entire thread. If you are a Republican, you'll get a good laugh out of the whole thing. It's amazing that Democrats spend so much time and energy on shooting each other in the foot.

Pro: maybe Democrats *have* had a bit of trouble closing the deal...

And recognizing that fact is the first step towards fixing it, as commenter **chicago jeff** observed.

---

[45] http://www.dailykos.com/story/2006/9/18/184750/636

[46] Ibid.

[47] http://www.dailykos.com/storyonly/2006/9/17/21151/0231

HE BELIEVES IN A STRONG NATIONAL DEFENSE.

In actuality Obama takes a rather unexceptionable position on defense spending, i.e. we need to be strong but we need to be smart about it. However, some newspapers reported the story as "**Obama chides other Democrats on defense.**" If this were true, it would be a pretty potent factoid to deploy for or against an Obama candidacy for President. Of course, it is not true.

The rumor got started this way, in the lede of an AP article on Obama's Sep. 18 speech to Iowa Democrats:

> Sen. Barack Obama, D-Ill., warned Democratic activists Sunday that the party must take a tougher stance on national security if it wants to succeed in the November elections.[48]

Unfortunately, as dailykos blogger **leevank** meticulously documented, Obama actually no such thing.

> Fortunately, C-SPAN now has the video of the entire speech posted, and it can be this link to the video from C-SPAN.[49] (It's the link entitled "American Politics: Sen Obama and Ann Richards. Sen. Obama's speech begins a couple of minutes into the video, after John Warner's brief remarks.)
>
> I urge every Kossack to watch Obama's entire speech, and see whether they see anything that could remotely be characterized in the manner that the AP story describes the speech. I see a very tough, hard-hitting speech that attacks the Bush administration on both domestic and national security issues.

As leevank pointed out, six other articles reporting on the same event failed to mention the mythical attack on other Democrats.

---

[48] http://news.yahoo.com/s/ap/20060918/ap_on_el_ge/obama_democrats_5

[49] http://c-span.org/Search/basic.asp?BasicQueryText=obama&SortBy=date

- Chicago Tribune[50]

- Southern Illinoisian[51]

- Radio Iowa[52]

- The Daily Iowan[53]

- Des Moines Register[54]

- Waterloo-Cedar Falls Courier[55]

---

[50] http://www.chicagotribune.com/news/nationworld/chi-0609180185sep18,1,7093952.story?coll=chi-newsnationworld-hed&ctrack=1&cset=true

[51] http://www.southernillinoisan.com/articles/2006/09/18/top/17587158.txt

[52] http://www.radioiowa.com/gestalt/go.cfm?objectid=E1594088-E5A8-4596-930A3CCF490BB7EE

[53] http://media.www.dailyiowan.com/media/storage/paper599/news/2006/09/18/Metro/Obama.Wows.Steak.Fry-2281918.shtml?sourcedomain=www.dailyiowan.com&MIIHost=media.collegepublisher.com

[54] http://www.desmoinesregister.com/apps/pbcs.dll/article?AID=2006609180337

[55] http://www.wcfcourier.com/articles/2006/09/18/news/politics/017137e1c577514e862571ed0043145a.txt

WHAT PEOPLE THINK ABOUT HIM

THE ILLINOIS STATE COMPTROLLER THINKS OBAMA SHOULD RUN IN 2008

Kicking off the bandwagon in September 2006.[56]

CHICAGO — In a highly unusual move, State Comptroller Daniel Hynes Thursday urged U.S. Sen. Barack Obama to run for the presidency in 2008.

At a news conference, Hynes called Obama the "man for these times," "awe-inspiring" and a "phenomenon" and said he hopes to spark a national movement to encourage the freshman senator to announce his candidacy....

Hynes said that he hadn't discussed the presidential election with Obama until Thursday, when he called the senator 10 minutes before he made his announcement to the press. He also wrote Obama a three-page letter urging him to run.

In a statement from his office, Obama said he was flattered by Hynes' public announcement, but he currently has no plans to run in the 2008 presidential election.[57]

Pro: the Comptroller of Illinois is for Obama in 2008!

Feel the love, Barry. Dan Hynes thinks you're The Man.

Con: the Comptroller of Illinois is for Obama is 2008!

Woo. The *comptroller?* Of *Illinois?* Well, if the *comptroller* of *Illinois* is in favor of Obama for President, it must be a good idea.

---

[56] http://news.google.com/news?sourceid=navclient-ff&ie=UTF-8&rlz=1B2GGGL_enUS177US177&q=barack%20obama&sa=N&tab=wn

[57] http://www.suburbanchicagonews.com/beaconnews/city/2_1_AU15_OBAMA_S10915.htm

ILLINOIS VOTERS THINK HE SHOULD RUN FOR PRESIDENT, SOONER OR LATER.

The Barack Obama for president bandwagon has hit Illinois, but voters are split on when the freshman U.S. senator should get in the driver's seat.

A quarter of voters want the South Side Democrat to seek the White House in 2008, and another 38 percent think he should wait until a later presidential year, according to a Chicago Sun-Times/NBC5 Poll.[58]

Pro: sixty percent of Illinois voters think Obama is "Presidential timber."

You've got to have a secure base. Remember, Al Gore lost Tennessee in 2000. **What a loser!**

Con: my *mom* probably thinks *I* should run for President, sooner or later.

Saying someone should run in "a later" President year is like saying you'd like to go out with them "sometime." Like when Hell freezes over...

Pro: this was based on an official *poll!*

The poll was paid for by the *Chicago Sun-Times* and MSNBC5.

Con: the poll was paid for the *The Chicago Sun-Times* and MSNBC5.

Being validated by a local news poll is like being validated by **Ron Burgundy**.

---

[58] http://www.suntimes.com/output/elect/cst-nws-pollside18.html

SALON THINKS HE SHOULD RUN IN '08.

> Barack Obama made a speech Thursday night in Louisville, Ky., before 5,000 cheering Democrats, and he got little more than a nice write-up in the Louisville Courier-Journal. Obama made a similar speech here Sunday afternoon to 3,000 party activists at the biggest event on the Iowa Democratic calendar -- **and the electric response among the press** was that the first-term Illinois senator is all but running for president in 2008.[59]

Pro: the media would support an Obama candidacy...

Despite the earnest debate about whether there is a liberal or a conservative bias to today's news institutions, **let's get real**: Obama makes incredible copy, and, even if **many** editors and most publishers are **Republican pigs**, there are huge numbers of liberal reporters who will regard Obama '08 as the second coming of, well, FDR, or maybe Jimmy Stewart:

> The faces in the crowd radiated a rapt intensity that you see in patriotic movies from the 1930s and 1940s but rarely in real life.[60]

Pro: he can create a media frenzy at will.

> When a local reporter discovers I'm from a publication far away, he asks if he can interview me about why *I'm* interested in Obama. This is what following the freshman senator has become: a small meta-chronicle of hysteria. It's like going to view the Mona Lisa at the Louvre. All you see are the backs of people's heads.[61]

---

[59] *Salon,* "Obama in '08," Walter Shapiro, September 18, 2006.

[60] *Ibid.*

[61] *New York,* "Dreaming of Obama," Jennifer Senior, October 2, 2006, http://newyorkmetro.com/news/politics/21681/index.html

Con: the media will support an Obama candidacy … until his first significant error.

At which point they will tear him to shreds **like rabid hyenas on cocaine-laced meth** tearing apart an especially cute and cuddly version of young Simba in *The Lion King*.

Pro: he's the most promising rookie in the class of '08.

Two years after his stirring keynote address at the convention in Boston, many Democrats already regard Obama as the greatest natural talent in the post-Clinton party. As Iowa attorney general Tom Miller said to me shortly after Obama left the stage, "A great speech. You can't beat charisma."[62]

Con: what if he blows out his arm?

What surprised me as I talked to random Iowans at the steak fry, though, was a palpable worry that Obama might lose his gilt-edged glow if he sought the nomination too soon in his career.

Pro: if not now, when?

When an almost equally junior senator named John Edwards was debating whether to run for president in 2004 or seek reelection to the Senate and save the White House dreams for another year, one of the most potent questions raised by his political advisors was, "What are you going to learn with four more years in the Senate that you don't know now?"[63]

Con: if not now, how about when you're qualified for the job?

With four more years in the Senate, Obama might learn something about how the Executive Branch operates, and how to oversee it.

Pro: Bush has executive experience, and look how well *that's* worked out.

---

[62] *Ibid.*

[63] *Ibid.*

BILL CLINTON THINKS HE SHOULD RUN – JUST NOT IN '08.

According to *The New Yorker's* David Remnick, Bill Clinton has been doing a bit of well-timed pre-emptive positioning against the faint possibility of an Obama candidacy disrupting **HillaryFest 2008:**

> `Later that night, Clinton invited everyone travelling with him, along with the heads of the foundation staff in Rwanda, up to his suite for dinner. At first, he talked about his meetings with some of the survivors of the genocide, but pretty quickly he seemed eager to talk about more distant subjects: wind and solar power, the frustrations with the Gore campaign in 2000 ("But he won, that's crystal clear to me"), and Barack Obama, who he thinks has the intelligence and the toughness necessary to be President **but has to be careful about running too soon-"like John Edwards."**[64]

As commenter Bill K pithily observed,

> I notice Bill didn't tell Barack Obama it was too early to run for Vice-President...![65]

Pro: if Bill Clinton thinks Obama is intelligent and tough enough to be President, that's a pretty high compliment.

Whatever his faults, the 42d President of the United States is an intelligent and tough-minded politican, and a shrewd judge of character.

Con: No token Obamas, pls.

Commenter Bill K. went on to suggest "**Gore-Obama '08!** [66]" Do we really want to see that? **I don't.**

---

[64] http://blogs.suntimes.com/sweet/2006/09/president_clinton_wa rns_barack.html

[65] Ibid.

[66] Ibid.

If all Obama is going to do is to be a token black and a token "exciting" candidate, a la John Edwards I'd rather he stayed home. I hope he feels the same way.

HE'S OPRAH'S "FAVORITE GUY."

Oprah Winfrey said on Monday's "Larry King Live" that she liked Sen. Barack Obama for president, dubbing him her "favorite guy."

Winfrey, asked about a Kansas City man who is trying to promote her for president, advised him to get behind Obama, her fellow Chicagoan.

"Take your energy and put it in Barack Obama. That's what I would say," Winfrey said, according to an advance transcript.

"Is that your favorite?" King asked. "That would be my favorite guy," she responded.[67]

Pro: how much advertising money would it take to match the value of an appearance on Oprah?

If you aren't independently wealthy (a la John Kerry), being Oprah's "favorite guy" has to run a close second.

Con: Obama's sewn up the all-important "billionaires who can't pump gas" vote.

---

[67] *Chicago Sun-Times,* September 26, 2006,
http://www.suntimes.com/news/metro/72231,CST-NWS-oside26.article

HOWARD FINEMAN CALLS HIM "A HUMAN EMBODIMENT OF UNITY."

Howard Fineman of *Newsweek* is in **loooovvvee:**

> **Is it fair to say that you are a human embodiment of the kind of unity** you think people are hungering for?
>
> I don't know that I am a human embodiment of it. I think that probably it helps that I've got pieces of everybody in me.

What an insane question.

Pro: holy crap! The media love this guy!

Con: I wish he had said "no, are you crazy?"

BILL O'REILLY THINKS OBAMA IS CAGEY.

Newsweek interviewed Bill O'Reilly about his latest book, *Culture Warrior.*

> DARMAN: Your book champions "traditionalists" and scolds "secular progressives." Are there Democratic traditionalists?
>
> O'REILLY: Joseph Lieberman, John F. Kennedy, Robert F. Kennedy.
>
> DARMAN: So two deceased Democrats and one who lost his party's primary.
>
> O'REILLY: OK, maybe Evan Bayh. **Maybe Barack Obama. From what I can see of him he does have traditional beliefs. But I could be wrong because he's cagey.** [68]

Con: *Bill O'Reilly?* **If you're Bill O'Reilly, practically anyone looks cagey.**

Pro: anyone who confuses Bill O'Reilly must be doing something right.

---

[68] http://mediamatters.org/items/200609250001

SOME ISRAELI EXPERTS DON'T TRUST HIM.

The Israeli newspaper *Haaretz* convened a panel of experts to assess and track 2008 Presidential candidates and evaluate them on "whom they consider best for Israel." In the first round of voting in September 2006, Obama came in dead last, **eighteenth** out of a field of eighteen, with an average score of 4.88 out of a possible 10. [69]

(The preferred candidate from the Department of Wishful Thinking was Rudy Giuliani, who scored an 8.75 with this group of experts who seem to have forgotten the **"Nixon to China" rule** that it sometimes takes a hawk to reverse a well established policy, such as, let's say, American support for Israel. Of course, the Israeli experts may be remembering that the **Sadat goes to Jerusalem** ploy didn't work out too well for their neighbor Anwar Sadat, who was assassinated not long after his heroic "good for Israel" visit.)

Haaretz correspondent Shmuel Rosner commented:

> Some might suggest that[the low ranking] is because he is an African-American, and the panel is suspicious about the prospect of a candidate from the African-American community, which is not generally perceived as being particularly Israel-friendly. Others, however, might suggest that it has more to do with his inexperience and the fact that he is unlikely to ultimately be a serious contender this time round.
>
> My sense is that the panel's ranking of Obama will change in the coming months.[70]

In fact, the *Haaretz* page devoted to Obama notes that during the 2006 Israel-Lebanon war was careful to defend Israel's right to defend itself against Hezbollah's incursions and missile attacks.[71]

---

[69] http://www.haaretz.com/hasen/pages/rosnerPage.jhtml

[70] http://www.haaretz.com/hasen/pages/ShArt.jhtml?itemNo=758697

[71] http://www.haaretz.com/hasen/pages/ShArt.jhtml?itemNo=756712

Pro: Obama will be uniquely positioned to resolve the Israeli-Arab conflict.

THE ARGUMENT IN FAVOR OF PRESIDENT BARACK OBAMA is that a liberal Democrat who is not trusted by Israeli experts is exactly what the United States and the world needs. Only by treating Palestinian rights with dignity and by forcing Israel to accept a much-reduced status in a two-state solution can the Middle East problem be resolved. When President Obama is inaugurated he will inevitably enjoy a great upwelling of good will in Europe and the Third World. Why waste this precious political capital with a temporizing business-as-usual policy?

Surely President Obama will be able to secure unprecedented support from grateful European allies and an Arab that suddenly finds the United States taking its grievances seriously. A Democratic Administration will not repeat George Bush's mistake of alienating the entire world.

Con: Who are you kidding? President Obama will be widely detested in the Muslim World.

YOU SEEM TO BE FORGETTING, FRED, that, if President Obama comes to power, it will surely be on the basis of a campaign that cleverly blends authentic Christian religiosity with an inspiring message of tolerance and diversity. Unfortunately, this message runs exactly opposite to the core values of fundamentalist Islam.

Similarly, it is clear that even the most liberal President Obama imaginable will not take the vile? idiotic? Richard Cohen position that "Israel is a mistake."[72] Assuming that President Obama continues to support Israel's right to exist, his policy will, ultimately, do' nothing to improve Israeli-Arab relations, because Arabs will never accept the existence of the state of Israel.

---

[72] Richard Cohen,"Hunker Down with History," *Washington Post,* July 18, 2006. http://www.washingtonpost.com/wp-dyn/content/article/2006/07/17/AR2006071701154.html

Alan Keyes thinks Jesus Christ wouldn't vote for Obama.

Alan Keyes, familiar to political junkies as a perennial and extremely conservative black Republican candidate for President, ran against Obama in the 2004 Illinois senate race.

> Keyes, who has focused his campaign on abortion, said that his statement about whom Jesus would vote for was based on Obama's pro-choice votes in the Illinois Senate.
>
> "Christ would not stand idly by while an infant child in that situation died," Keyes said. "And I'm not the only person, obviously, who thinks if you are a representative of me, I cannot vote for you if you would ignore the dignity and claims of that child's life. So, yes, I did respond quite logically -- you'll see it's quite logical, right -- with the conclusion that Christ would not vote for Barack Obama, because Barack Obama has voted to behave in a way that it is inconceivable for Christ to have behaved."[73]

Con: Keyes makes a logical argument.

I agree that Jesus Christ wouldn't vote for a murderer.

Pro: Keyes makes a loony argument.

I am opposed to abortion. I vote against strongly pro-choice candidates. Even so, I still think Keyes is making a loony argument here. Why do I think that? I'm not sure I can come up with a definitive explanation why the word "loony" comes to mind, but here's a first cut:

- It's **presumptuous** to claim to know the mind of Jesus Christ.

- It's **anachronistic** to imagine Jesus Christ voting in a 2004 state election.

---

[73] NBC5 News, September 7, 2004.
http://www.nbc5.com/politics/3712293/detail.html

- It's **self-defeating** for Keyes to make an argument that only appeals to devout anti-abortion Christians, who are, alas, an electoral minority in Illinois and the rest of the country.

The first and the third bullets are the ones that feel as if they're the most authentic source for the "loony" feeling that emanates from Keyes' remarks.

Con: with enemies like these, who needs friends?

Obama was lucky to run against a self-defeating candidate in 2004. Before we start talking about Obama for President, let's see him win a *contested* election or two.

He inspires hope among Democrats.

There are lots of reasons why activists seemed to like Obama, but they all came down to this: **Hope**. Hope for their party - this guy looks like a winner. And hope for the country. A lot of Democrats are tired and angry at what's been happening. Before Sunday's event, one activist told me privately that she wants Obama to run for president because electing him would be one way for the United States to repair the damage done to its reputation around the world during the Bush presidency. She cited as evidence the warm reception Obama got on his recent trip to Africa.

Obama offers them a promise of something fresh, uplifting and different. Most of the other candidates can't do that.[74]

Pro: it's time for Democrats to be happy!

Pro: it's time for other countries to be happy!

Con: who cares if Democrats and Africans are happy?

---

[74] *Des Moines Register*, "What triggers the big buzz around Obama? It's hope," by David Yepsen, September 21, 2006.

SOME "EXPERTS" THINK HE'S TOO POPULAR TO BE PRESIDENT.

That's the somewhat loopy thesis offered by Kevin McDermott of the *St. Louis Post-Dispatch* after talking to a pollster or two.

> "It's a cliche, but it's true: The higher you go, the harder you fall," warned pollster Del Ali of Research 2000, which conducted a poll for the St. Louis Post-Dispatch last month that showed Obama with an unheard-of 70 percent approval rating among Illinoisans.[75]

Pro: we should all have such problems.

If that's the best that Obama skeptics can come up with, he might as well run in '08.

Con: the politics of Presidential elections is, unfortunately, all about expectation management.

Like it or not, the media only know one way to write national campaign stories, in terms of **the gap between expectations and performance.**

> One rule of thumb in politics is to keep expectations low so that any mistake the politician makes looks smaller while any accomplishment looks bigger. For Obama, sitting on a runaway train of gushing publicity, that kind of "expectation control" has become impossible.[76]

---

[75] *The Myrtle Beach Sun-News,* September 18, 2006.

[76] Ibid.

PRESIDENT OBAMA WILL IMPROVE OUR RELATIONS WITH THE MUSLIM WORLD.

It's possible that electing President with a Muslim last name and a Muslim father will improve our relations with the Muslim world. Here are a couple of **bass-ackward** arguments on that score.

Pro: We need to be more popular in the Muslim World.

According to numerous studies such as the Pew Global Research surveys, American policies are highly unpopular in the Muslim world and are blamed for most of the region's ills. We need to be more popular with these people who are angry at us.

Con: The Muslim world needs to be more popular with us.

Who cares if we're unpopular in the Muslim world? They need to be more like us.

Pro: President Obama will be uniquely positioned to deal with the principal foreign-policy challenge of the early 21st century, the Muslim World.

> "I WILL GO TO PAKISTAN," Senator Obama pledged. The dramatic gesture, reminiscent of Dwight Eisenhower's pledge to go to Korea, tilted the balance in a close race. Millions of patriotic Americans had never forgotten. that Osama Bin Ladin was responsible for three thousand American deaths. The newly inaugurated President Obama's visit to Pakistan, where he scattered ashes from the World Trade Center at the footsteps of a mosque, is widely credited with the change in Pakistani sentiment that led to Bin Ladin's capture in 2009.[77]

---

[77] Wikipedia, Capture of Bin Ladin, January 4, 2001, http://www.wikipedia.com/capture_of_bin_ladin.

Con: the principal foreign policy challenge of the early 21st Century is China, and Obama brings nothing to the table there.

WHOOPS! While we were focusing on militant Islam, **China was busy becoming the world's largest industrial power.** President Obama, with his scanty foreign policy knowledge, business experience, and cumbersome Democratic "netroots" legacy, proved to be poorly equipped to navigate the challenging world of global economic competition.[78]

---

[78] *The Rise and Fall of The American Empire*, Niall Phillips, China State Publishing Company, 2017.

HE'S AN OPINION DRIVER!

According to the HuffPo imitators at Hotsoup.com, who announced on Sep. 21:

> Washington DC — SEPTEMBER 20, 2006 — **HOTSOUP.com®**, the first online community to unite Opinion Drivers from across the spectrum, today announced that **Senator Barack Obama**, advisor to President Bush Mary Matalin, former White House press secretary Scott McLellan, producer/director Davis Guggenheim, and cancer survivor and mother of two Heidi Boynton will participate in discussions when the community goes live next month.

> According to **Senator Obama,** "Americans are tired of the spin they get from too many leaders today. If an online community can give grassroots opinion leaders a platform for smart, civil debate, it will fill a huge void in today's politics."

> HOTSOUP.com aims to give the public a voice in this country's decision making process; to move public conversation beyond the spin and build a forum where Opinion Drivers will exchange ideas and voice opinions. Within the community, grassroots Opinion Drivers will be joined by the biggest names in politics, business, religion and culture to discuss the important issues of the day.[79]

Pro: Hotsoup.com has worthy goals.

> HOTSOUP.com is the first online community that joins Opinion Drivers from across the spectrum. Harnessing the power of social networking technology, it connects well-known influencers from the worlds of politics, business, entertainment, and industry with influencers who drive opinion on the grassroots and community level. **By uniting these individuals in conversation and debate, HOTSOUP.com breaks through the polarization in this country, allowing for a healthy exchange of ideas and opinions.** HOTSOUP.com was created by a diverse team of professionals from politics, high-tech and journalism.[80]

---

[79] http://hotsoup.com/press/Obama%20Matalin%20et%20al%20FINAL.doc

[80] Ibid.

Con: "opinion driver" is a horrible term.

The original term was "opinion leader" and it was applied to "regular guys" who were influential members of their community without necessarily being in official positions of power. "Opinion driver" has exactly the wrong "top-down" connotation that sounds like someone herding a bunch of sheep.

Con: Obama is probably going to be represented by a staffer who can (barely) pass the Turing test.

Do you seriously think Obama is going to be hunched over the keyword composing his own thoughts? Maybe for the first post as a favor to old friends, but after the first post, I visualize a staff aide with a hefty supply of Obama verbiage ready to cut and paste.

HE'S A MULTIPLIER, NOT A DIVIDER.

This clanky neologism was coined by Robert S. McElvaine of the Jackson, Mississippi *Clarion-Ledger*.

> The last thing our nation needs in 2008 is another 50-50 election of bitter red/blue division. What America needs is a leader who practices the politics of multiplication rather than division.
>
> The person who has the greatest potential to be the Multiplier has just returned from a highly successful visit to Africa and will be speaking next Sunday in Iowa, site of the opening caucuses in the 2008 presidential selection process: Sen. Barack Obama of Illinois.[81]

Pro: America wants a President who will bring us together.

The current highly partisan atmosphere is tiresome in the extreme. McElvaine is right, we need a unifier.

Con: America voted for a President who divided us.

Talk is cheap. In 2004 the majority of us voted for arguably the most divisive President in American history. It would appear that McElvaine is wrong: we don't want a multiplier, we want a divider, and that's what we've got.

Pro: A multiplier is electable.

McElvaine cleverly argues that:

> Obama would win almost all of the Democratic base that voted for Al Gore and John Kerry and would be very likely to carry Ohio, giving him an Electoral College majority.

Con: An African-American Multiplier is not electable.

McElvaine concedes that

---

[81] Robert McElwaine, *The Clarion-Ledger*, September 13, 2006. http://www.clarionledger.com/apps/pbcs.dll/article?AID=/20060913/OPINION/609130311/1285

A significant fraction of the American electorate would vote against any black candidate.

Is America ready for a black President? We're not even ready for a Jewish President or a woman President. What makes anyone think Barack Obama is electable?

Pro: We're better than that.

I believe it. So does Robert McElvaine, both on practical grounds:

the prospect of the first black president would be likely to produce a phenomenon similar to the first free election in South Africa. Blacks would register in unprecedented numbers and the percentage of black registrants who actually vote would soar. Add this upsurge in black voters to the minority of whites in the South who vote Democratic and many Southern states - including Mississippi - could become winnable for the Democrats.

And on moral ones:

The symbolism of the first African-American president being inaugurated less than a month before the nation celebrates the bicentennial of the Great Emancipator should be enough to dampen the eyes even of political cynics.

Well said, sir.

WHO HE IS AS A MAN

HE'S LUCKY.

Howard Fineman of *Newsweek* asked Obama a good question and got a lucky answer:

> **Q.** The reaction you get around the country is remarkable. Why are people reacting to you the way they are?
>
> **A.** It's always hard to stand outside yourself and know what it is that people are reacting to. Some **of it is just dumb luck.**[82]

What are we to make of this answer?

Pro: luck sticks.

Con: no, it doesn't.

He's a good orator, but he's not Winston Churchill yet.

Con: he may sound too smart to win.

David Mendell commented in the *Chicago Tribune:*

> It wasn't that Obama's appearance was anything close to a flop, or that his speech left Iowans cold. **Rather, he left them in deep thought.**
>
> Coming after years of red-meat speeches from hard-charging Democrats such as John Edwards and Howard Dean and home-state hero Harkin, Obama's professorial prose more evoked **the cerebral Adlai Stevenson.**
>
> Deep thinking is ideal for the Harvard classroom and Cambridge coffeehouse, where one presumes Obama excelled while at Harvard Law. But would it translate into votes at Iowa caucus time?
>
> ... Wesley's husband, Ron, said he enjoyed Obama's address but thought **the former constitutional law professor came across as a bit too intellectual for his taste.**[83]

---

[82] Newsweek, September 25, 2006.
http://msnbc.msn.com/id/14961215/site/newsweek/page/2/

[83] *Chicago Tribune,* "Looking beyond Obama-mania: Is he ready yet?", September 24, 2006, by David Mendell.

Con: sometimes he's (gasp) a leetle boring.

Mendell thoughtfully explained:

> .. truth is, Obama turned in a rare mediocre performance in Indianola. He spoke for nearly 40 minutes, longer than usual on the stump. He stitched together bits of previous speeches, particularly portions of his 2004 campaign speech, and then wrapped it all up with a thoughtful condemnation of the Bush administration.
>
> The excessive length occasionally gave his address the feel of a lecture rather than a hard-core stump speech. ...

Pro: he can only get better.

Give the stump speech a few hundred times, and it'll be fine.

Pro: maybe we need someone who expects more from us.

What's wrong with someone who makes us think?

Pro: he's only being strategically boring.

The *Tribune's* David Mendell theorized:

> In addition, the lack of a new, finely honed speech in this high-profile setting also might signal that we should take Obama at his word, that he is not yet seriously considering a White House bid, despite hype to the contrary.[84]

Con: he's proud of being boring.

> One thing I'm proud of is that very rarely will you hear me simplify the issues.[85]
>
> . "These either/or formulations are wearisome," he says. "They're not useful. The reality outstrips the mental categories we're operating in."[86]

---

[84] Ibid.

[85] *Newsweek*, September 25, 2006.

[86] *New York*, "Dreaming of Obama," by Jennifer Senior, October 2, 2006 http://newyorkmetro.com/news/politics/21681/index1.html

HE'S AN ADMIRER OF DICK CHENEY.

As he proved at the Gridiron Club dinner in March 2006.

> Mr. Vice President, I know you came here expecting to be a target, which, it turns out, may prove easier for you than shooting at one. But I do want to thank you: for years, we Democrats have succeeded in doing little more than shooting ourselves in the foot. You've taught us a valuable lesson: aim higher.
>
> There's probably only one person more sick of these jokes than you... and that's your wife. It's an honor to share this stage with Lynne Cheney -- a great personage in her own right. Scholar. Author. A few years ago she wrote a book called, "Telling the Truth, or as they call it in the Vice President's office, "Telling the Truth-24 hours later
>
> ... I also enjoyed that biathlon, where they ski and shoot at the same time. Probably not your sport, Mr. Vice President..[87]

Pro: anyone brave enough to poke fun at Cheney deserves to be President.

> The truth is, I'm terrified to be here. Not because you're such a tough audience, but because they're serving drinks, I'm standing about 30 yards from the Vice President, and...Mr. Vice President this is too easy![88]

---

[87] http://blogs.suntimes.com/sweet/2006/03/best_of_gridiron_obama_lynne_c.html

[88] Ibid.

HE'S HUMBLE.

"I want to thank you for all the generous advance coverage you've given me in anticipation of a successful career. When I actually do something, we'll let you know."

About that book, some folks thought it was a little presumptuous to write an autobiography at the age of 33, but people seemed to like it. So now I'm working on volume two-the Senate Months

My Remarkable Journey from 99th in Seniority to 98th.

(With an introduction by Nelson Mandela.).[89]

The last time I played [basketball] was actually in Djibouti, with [U.S.] troops. I was terrific for the first five minutes.[90]

---

[89] http://blogs.suntimes.com/sweet/2006/03/best_of_gridiron
_obama_lynne_c.html

[90] *Newsweek*, September 25, 2006.

HE LIKES SPORTS.

Pro: he 's got game.

Someone I know played basketball with you at Harvard Law School, and he complimented you on your game. He said you ran the floor and shared the ball. How would you describe your game?

I was a slasher—somewhere between Alan Iverson and LeBron James, but keep in mind that the gym in law school was pretty short, shorter than regulation. [91]

Con: can a black man who likes basketball become President?

Sure, why not? It worked for Bill Bradley.

Pro: he's a Michigan fan.

Often, Colvin said, he and the senator have heart-to-heart conversations. Topics cover family history, what shaped Obama's beliefs and political actions and even Michigan football.

"He was pretty enthusiastic about Michigan beating Notre Dame," Colvin said. [92]

Pro: case closed. This guy's on the side of the angels.

---

[91] Newsweek, September 26, 2006.

[92] *Michigan Daily*, "U. Michigan alumnus works as personal assistant to Barack Obama," Dave Mekelburg, September 26, 2006.

HE HAS ECLECTIC TASTES IN MUSIC.

Colvin said Obama has an eclectic taste in music, listening to everything from Indonesian flute music to OutKast to Motown.[93]

Pro: Motown.

George Bush doesn't listen to much Motown.

Con: Indonesian *flute* music?

That's not going to get him many votes.

---

[93] Ibid.

HE HAS A GOOD SENSE OF HUMOR.

Pro: a sense of humor is an important quality in a President.

Humorous Presidents	Humorless Presidents
John F. Kennedy	Richard Nixon
Bill Clinton	George H.W. Bush
Ronald Reagan	Gerald Ford
George W. Bush	James Buchanan

Con: Presidents with a sense of humor tend to be dangerous adventurers.

John F. Kennedy (Cuba)

Bill Clinton (Monica)

Ronald Reagan (Star Wars)

George W. Bush (Iraq)

Pro: he inspires other Democrats to be funny.

After Obama's stellar performance at the Iowa Steak Fry:

> Senator TOM HARKIN (Democrat, Iowa): Well, I just thought, you know,
> `Here's Iowa. Why not try the kid next door, you know, give him a chance?
> No one knows who he is. Highlight him a little bit.` I'm just kidding. Everybody
> knows Barack Obama.[94]

---

[94] CBS Evening News, September 17, 2006.

85

He's funny for DC.

Here are some terrific funny-for-DC jokes from the Gridiron Club dinner. F

You know, The Gridiron Club is an aging institution with a long, proud history, known today primarily for providing a forum for jokes. To some, that may sound like the Democratic Party.

You hear this constant refrain from our critics that Democrats don't stand for anything. That's really unfair. We DO stand for anything.

Some folks say the answer for the Democratic Party is to stop being so calculating, and start standing up for principle. In fact, Harry Reid's appointed a task force to study this option.

But really, they say our party doesn't have ideas? We have ideas.

Take John Edwards. He's leading a new war on poverty... from his Chapel Hill estate. And he's educating us. I had no idea there was so much poverty in New Hampshire![95]

---

[95] http://blogs.suntimes.com/sweet/2006/03/best_of_gridiron_obama_ lynne_c.html

BUT HE KNOWS WHEN NOT TO BE FUNNY.

At the Gridiron Club dinner, he took the time to make one serious point.

> Hey, it's been great fun to be a part of this tonight. But before I go, I want to say a few words about the work you do.
>
> For a democracy to succeed and flourish, people must have full and free access to information about what's going on in their world and, yes, in their government.
>
> The framers of the Constitution understood that, which is why the very first amendment deals with the indispensable freedoms of speech and press. Those rights, those freedoms, the access to information citizens absolutely require in a democratic society are no less important today.
>
> Pursuing that information is not always easy. Sometimes you meet resistance from powerful institutions that would sooner operate in secrecy. And sometimes, as in Iraq, you literally risk your lives to keep the American people informed.
>
> Tonight, even as we laugh together, I want to thank you for that important and often courageous work and extend my prayers to those journalists and their families who have made and continue to make great sacrifices to fulfill this essential mission.[96]

Well said, sir.

---

[96] http://blogs.suntimes.com/sweet/2006/03/best_of_gridiron_obama_lynne_c.html

Nɪᴍʙʟᴇ Bᴏᴏᴋs LLC

INDEX

COLOPHON

This book was produced using Microsoft Word and Adobe Acrobat. The cover was produced using The Gimp 2.0.2 with Ghostscript. The cover font is Constantia. The spine is Verdana.

Heading fonts and the body text inside the book are in Constantia, chosen because it is a nimble-looking font that is new enough to be fresh on the eyes. Quotations are in Consolas, a fixed width font chosen for similar reasons.

The American Heritage® Dictionary of the English Language, Fourth Edition,copyright © 2000 by Houghton Mifflin Company defines col·o·phon as follows:

> An ancient Greek city of Asia Minor northwest of Ephesus. It was famous for its cavalry.

Along the same lines, Webster's Revised Unabridged, copyright 1996, 1998, MICRA, Inc.:

> \Col"o*phon\ (k[o^]l"[-o]*f[o^]n), n. [L. colophon finishing stroke, Gr. kolofw`n; cf. L. culmen top, collis hill. Cf. Holm.] An inscription, monogram, or cipher, containing the place and date of publication, printer's name, etc., formerly placed on the last page of a book.

I always like to find an appropriate finishing stroke for each book that I publish. In this case, what could be more appropriate than these wonderful words from Barack Obama's finest moment, his keynote speech at the 2004 Democratic Convention?

> We worship an awesome God in the Blue States...

ited in the United States
32LVS00004B/253-255

9 780978 813802